THE MURDERS
IN THE RUE MORGUE

There are many famous detectives in the world of books – Philip Marlowe in Los Angeles, Vic Warshawski in Chicago, Inspector Morse in Oxford, and of course, the great Sherlock Holmes in London. But before any of these, there was Monsieur Auguste Dupin in Paris.

He was not a policeman, and not really a detective either. He was a quiet young man, who loved books and reading. But he was clever, and he could understand many things that other people did not. He took a close interest in the horrible murders in the Rue Morgue, because there were no answers to the mystery. Who murdered the old lady and her daughter? Why were the murders so brutal? How did the murderer get out of the house? So many questions – and no answers.

'The secret,' said Auguste Dupin, 'is to ask the *right* questions. Then you will find the answers . . .'

OXFORD BOOKWORMS LIBRARY

Crime & Mystery

The Murders in the Rue Morgue

Stage 2 (700 headwords)

Series Editor: Jennifer Bassett
Founder Editor: Tricia Hedge
Activities Editors: Jennifer Bassett and Christine Lindop

EDGAR ALLAN POE

The Murders in the Rue Morgue

Retold by
Jennifer Bassett

Illustrated by
Chris Koelle

OXFORD UNIVERSITY PRESS

OXFORD
UNIVERSITY PRESS

Great Clarendon Street, Oxford ox2 6dp

Oxford University Press is a department of the University of Oxford.
It furthers the University's objective of excellence in research, scholarship,
and education by publishing worldwide in

Oxford New York

Auckland Cape Town Dar es Salaam Hong Kong Karachi
Kuala Lumpur Madrid Melbourne Mexico City Nairobi
New Delhi Shanghai Taipei Toronto

With offices in

Argentina Austria Brazil Chile Czech Republic France Greece
Guatemala Hungary Italy Japan Poland Portugal Singapore
South Korea Switzerland Thailand Turkey Ukraine Vietnam

OXFORD and OXFORD ENGLISH are registered trade marks of
Oxford University Press in the UK and in certain other countries

ISBN 978 0 19 479078 9

A complete recording of this Bookworms edition of
The Murders in the Rue Morgue is available.

Printed in China

ACKNOWLEDGEMENTS

Illustrated by: Chris Koelle/Portland Studios, Greenville, USA

Word count (main text): 6995 words

For more information on the Oxford Bookworms Library,
visit www.oup.com/elt/gradedreaders

CONTENTS

1

My friend Auguste Dupin

I met Monsieur Auguste Dupin while I was living in Paris during the spring and summer of 1839. This young Frenchman was from an old and famous family, but the family was now very poor and Dupin only had a little money to live on. He ate and drank very little, bought no clothes, and lived very quietly. Books were the love of his life, and in Paris it is easy to get books.

Our first meeting was in a small bookshop in the Rue

My first meeting with Auguste Dupin

Montmartre. We were looking for the same old book, and that is how our conversation began. We met again and again, and were soon very friendly.

He knew much more about books than I did. Conversation with a man like him was very helpful for my studies, and after a time we agreed to find a house and live there together for the time of my stay in Paris.

We found a house in a quiet street in the Faubourg St. Germain. It was a very old house, and was neither beautiful nor comfortable. But it was right for us, and our strange way of life.

We saw no visitors, had no friends, and lived only for the night. When morning came, we closed all the shutters on our windows, and in this half-light we spent the day reading, writing, or talking, until the true darkness came. Then we went out into the streets, and walked for hours among the wild lights and shadows of the crowded city.

During these night walks I learnt how clever my friend was. He could think so clearly and understood so much! He could read other people's thoughts as easily as writing on a wall. He often said, with a laugh, that people had windows in their faces and that he could see through them. Sometimes he read *my* thoughts in ways that surprised me very much.

One night we were walking down a long street near the Jardin du Luxembourg. We were both thinking, and for fifteen minutes we did not say a word. Then, suddenly, Dupin said:

'He cannot write tragedy, that's true. He's much better at writing his funny pieces for the newspaper.'

'Oh yes, I agree with that. He—' Then I stopped, astonished. 'Dupin,' I said, 'I do not understand. How could you possibly know that I was thinking about—?' Again, I stopped. Did Dupin really know who I was thinking about?

'About Chantilly,' Dupin said. 'You were saying to yourself that he was a good writer, but he cannot write tragedy.'

'Yes, that's true,' I said. 'I *was* thinking that. But tell me, please! How did you know?'

This Chantilly wrote for one of the Paris newspapers. He wrote about Paris and Parisians in a way that was both clever and very funny. But then he wrote a book, a long story about the ancient Greeks, and Phaedra, the wife of King Theseus. It was, everybody in Paris agreed, a very bad book.

'It was the apple-seller,' replied my friend. 'The apple-seller began the thoughts that took you to Chantilly and his book.'

'The apple-seller!' I said, astonished. 'But I don't know any apple-sellers.'

My friend was happy to explain. 'Some minutes ago we

passed an apple-seller, who was carrying a big box of apples on his head, taking them to the fruit market. He didn't see you, and you had to jump out of his way. There were holes in the street, and you turned your foot in one of these holes and nearly fell.'

'*You had to jump out of the apple-seller's way.*'

I remembered this now, but how did the apple-seller take us to Chantilly?

'You looked around,' my friend went on, 'and saw all the other holes and broken stones in the street, and then you looked up, a little angrily, to see the name of the street. You were thinking, I am sure, that it was a dangerous street to walk down in the dark, when you could not easily see the holes.

'Then we turned a corner into the Rue Racine. Here, the stones were new and unbroken, and you looked up, pleased, to find the name of this street. This name began a new thought. You smiled a little and shook your head. The famous Racine, who wrote a play about Phaedra in 1677, was a better writer than Chantilly will ever be. And you remembered that when Chantilly's book first came out, the bookshops called Chantilly "the new Racine". Everybody in Paris laughed at poor Chantilly because of that. I was sure that you were thinking of that when you smiled. And when you shook your head, I knew you were thinking of poor Chantilly's book.'

2

The murders

Not long after that night, we were looking through the *Gazette*, an evening newspaper, when we saw this:

TERRIBLE MURDERS

At about three o'clock this morning people living in the St. Roch Quarter were woken from sleep by a number of terrible screams. The screams came from the fourth floor of a house in the Rue Morgue, which belongs to a Madame L'Espanaye, and her daughter, Mademoiselle Camille L'Espanaye.

Eight or ten of the neighbours, and two policemen, ran to the house. There was no answer to their knocking, so they broke down the door. When they got into the house, the screams stopped, but while they were running up the stairs, they could hear two angry voices at the top of the house. When they arrived at the second floor, the voices stopped and everything was silent. The neighbours hurried from room to room but found nothing until they came to a large room at the back of the house on the fourth floor. This room was locked, with the key on the *inside*. They broke the door open and saw in the room something which was both horrible and astonishing.

Chairs and tables were broken and lay in pieces everywhere. There was one bed, and the mattress from it was now on the floor in the middle of the room. In front of the fireplace on the floor was a razor, with blood

They broke the door open.

on it, and some long grey hair, with blood on the end. Also on the floor were three large silver spoons, and two bags, which contained nearly four thousand francs in gold. A small strong-box was found under the mattress. It was open, with the key in the lock, and contained only a few old letters.

At first they thought there was nobody in the room, but when they looked up the chimney, they found (horrible to describe!) the dead body of the daughter, head downwards. It was difficult to pull the body out because the chimney was so narrow. The body was still warm. There were deep cuts on the face, and around the neck there were dark bruises and the marks of fingers.

The neighbours looked in all the other rooms, then went down into the small yard at the back of the house. There they found the dead body of Madame L'Espanaye. Her neck was very deeply cut, and when they tried to lift her, the head fell off. There were terrible bruises all over the body.

At the moment, the police say, there are no answers to this horrible mystery.

3

What the witnesses said

Dupin said nothing about these horrible murders that evening, but I knew he was interested, because the next day he opened the morning newspaper at once. There was a lot more about the mystery.

THE TRAGEDY IN THE RUE MORGUE

The police have talked to many people about this terrible tragedy. This is what witnesses have said, but nothing so far can explain the mystery in any way.

Pauline Dubourg, washerwoman

'I've known Madame and her daughter for three years. I do their washing for them and they pay very well. People say that the old lady was rich, but I don't know about that. I never saw anybody in the house when I went to get the washing or to take it back. I think they lived only on the fourth floor of the house.'

Pierre Moreau, shopkeeper

'I have lived all my life in this quarter. The house in the Rue Morgue belongs to Madame L'Espanaye, and she and her daughter have lived there for six years. Madame sometimes came into my shop, but I didn't see the daughter very often.

The two of them lived very quietly. In six years I never saw anybody go into their house except the postman and the doctor.'

Many other neighbours said the same thing. There were no visitors to the house, either friends or family. The shutters of the windows, front and back, were nearly always closed, except for the large back room on the fourth floor.

'I was the first up the stairs.'

Isodore Muset, policeman

'I was called to the house in the Rue Morgue at about three o'clock in the morning, and found twenty or thirty people at the front door. The screams from a person or people inside the house were very loud, but they stopped suddenly when we broke the front door down. I was the first up the stairs and when I reached the first floor, I could hear two angry voices, arguing loudly. One was a deep voice, the other high and shrill – a very strange voice. The deep voice was that of a Frenchman. I'm sure it wasn't a woman's voice. I could hear the words "*diable*" and "*Mon Dieu*". The shrill voice was a foreigner, perhaps a man or perhaps a woman. I couldn't hear any words, but the language was Spanish, I think.'

Henri Duval, a neighbour

'I agree with what Isodore Muset has said, except about the voices. The shrill voice was speaking in Italian – I'm sure it wasn't French. No, I don't know Italian myself, but I'm sure it sounded like Italian words. I knew Madame L. and her daughter, and it certainly wasn't either of their voices.'

Jan Odenheimer, kitchen worker

'I was walking past the house when I heard those long, terrible screams, and I was one of the people who went into the building and heard the voices on the stairs. I am from

Holland and don't speak French, but I'm sure the shrill voice was a man's voice – a Frenchman. I couldn't hear the words but the voice sounded angry and afraid. The deep voice said the word "*diable*" many times.'

Jules Mignaud, banker, Mignaud & Son

'Madame L'Espanaye opened an account at my bank eight years ago. She did not often take money out of her account, but three days before her death she took out four

'Mademoiselle L'Espanaye took one of the bags,
and then Madame took the other bag.'

thousand francs. This money was paid in gold, and a clerk took it to her house in the Rue Morgue.'

Adolphe Le Bon, bank clerk at Mignaud & Son
'On Monday, at about 12 o'clock, I went with Madame L'Espanaye to her home, carrying the four thousand francs in two bags. When Mademoiselle L'Espanaye opened the front door, she took one of the bags, and then Madame took the other bag. I said goodbye and left. There was nobody in the street at that time.'

William Bird, musician
'I'm an Englishman and I've lived in Paris for two years. I went into the house with the others and heard the voices on the stairs. The deep voice was that of a Frenchman – I remember hearing the words "*Mon Dieu*". I also heard a sound like people fighting. The shrill voice was very loud – louder than the deep one. It wasn't an Englishman's voice. I think it was a German, possibly a woman. No, I don't understand German.'

Several witnesses said that the door of the room on the fourth floor was locked, with the key on the inside. Everything was silent when they got up there, and when they broke the door open, they saw nobody in the room. The two windows were closed and fastened on the inside. The police have looked through the house very carefully – every room, every chimney, every corner – but they have found nothing. The witnesses do not agree about the time between hearing the voices and breaking open the door – some say it was three minutes, others say five minutes.

Alfonzo Garcia, cook

'I live in the Rue Morgue, but I come from Spain. I was too afraid to go upstairs, but I heard the voices arguing. The deep voice spoke in French, and the shrill voice was that of an Englishman. Yes, I'm sure. No, I can't speak English, but I know what it sounds like.'

Alberto Montani, fruit-seller

'I was one of the first up the stairs, and heard the voices – a Frenchman with a deep voice, saying something angry, and a shrill voice, which spoke quickly and unclearly. I think it was the voice of a Russian. Yes, I'm Italian. I've never spoken to a Russian person.'

Paul Dumas, doctor

'I was called to see the bodies at daybreak. Both of them were then lying in the room on the fourth floor. The young lady's body was bruised and cut all over when it was pushed up the chimney. The face was blue-black, the eyes were half out, and the neck was badly bruised, with deep red marks made by very strong fingers. These marks show

how she died. The mother's body was also horribly bruised, and all the bones of the right leg and arm were broken. How was this done? I don't know – perhaps by a heavy piece of wood like a table leg. A razor was used to cut the neck, and the head was no longer joined to the body. All this was done by a very strong person – a man, and a very strong one.'

There has never been a crime in Paris as mysterious as this one. How did the murderer or murderers escape from the house? The door to the room was locked, the windows were fastened. All the chimneys in the house are too narrow for a person to get through, there are no back stairs, and the door to the roof is very old and impossible to open. Whose voices did the witnesses hear? Why was the money left in the room? The police have no answers to these questions.

4

Auguste Dupin visits the Rue Morgue

Dupin read all this with great interest, and was the first to open the evening newspaper when it arrived.

He read silently, and then said, 'There is nothing new about the murders, but the police have arrested Adolphe Le Bon. Why, I don't know.' He looked at me. 'Well, my friend, what do *you* think about these murders?'

'It's a great mystery,' I said. 'It will be impossible, surely, ever to find this murderer.'

'We must not say "impossible" just because the police have done nothing,' said Dupin. 'The Parisian police do find the answers sometimes, but that is usually because of hard work, not because they are clever. Very often, you see, they don't think clearly. They look very hard at one or two things, but they don't *see* everything. You remember the saying, "They can't see the wood for the trees"? Well, sometimes it's important to stand back and look at the whole wood, and forget about the trees. Now, why don't we do a little detective work ourselves, and go round to the Rue Morgue? Adolphe Le Bon was once very helpful to me, and I would like to help him if I can. I know the police inspector, and I'm sure he will say that we can look round the house. So, shall we go?'

We went that same afternoon. We found the house easily because there were still people in the street looking up at the closed shutters. It was the usual kind of Parisian house, with nothing surprising about it. Before we went in, we walked up the street, turned down a narrow side street, and turned again to walk past the back of the building. Dupin

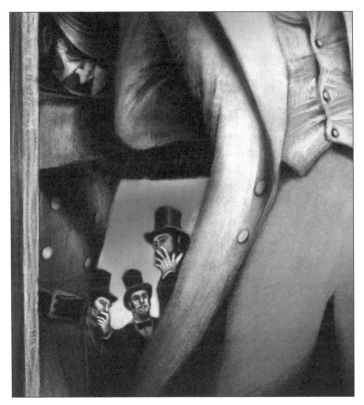

'*The police have arrested Adolphe Le Bon.*'

17

looked at everything – the ground, the walls, the windows, the shutters – but I did not know what he was looking for.

Then we went inside, and a policeman took us up to the fourth floor. The two dead bodies still lay there, with the broken chairs and tables all around them. Again, Dupin looked at everything – the room and the bodies – very carefully. Then we went down into the yard at the back. It was dark when we left the Rue Morgue, and on our way home Dupin went in for a moment to the office of one of the daily newspapers.

That evening my friend would not answer any of my questions. But the next day he suddenly asked me, 'Did you see anything *peculiar* in that house in the Rue Morgue?'

I don't know why, but his question made me afraid. 'No, nothing *peculiar*,' I said. 'Well, nothing more peculiar than what we both knew from the *Gazette*.'

'Neither the *Gazette* nor the police,' said Dupin, 'understand much about these murders. The police are puzzled by all the questions which they cannot answer. What was the motive for the murders? Why were the murders so brutal? Whose were the voices? How could these people get out of the house when the neighbours were running up the stairs? Why was everything broken in the room? Why was the girl's body up the chimney? Why did the old lady have so many broken bones?

'I'm afraid the police are making the mistake that many

Dupin looked at everything very carefully.

people make. They think that because the crime is so unusual, they can never explain it. But they are wrong. It is *more* helpful to have an unusual crime, because that will make us think harder, and ask the right questions, and in the end find the answer. We must not ask the question,

"What has happened?"; we must ask, "What has happened *that has never happened before*?" The answer to this mystery is not really difficult at all – I think I know it already.'

I looked at him, astonished, and could not say a word.

'I am now waiting,' he went on, 'for a person who is probably not the murderer himself, but who certainly knows something about the murders. He will arrive here – in this room – at any moment. I hope, and think, he will. And if he does come, it will be necessary to stop him leaving. Here are four guns, two for you and two for me. We both know how to use them if we have to.'

'If he does come, it will be necessary to stop him leaving.'

5

The mysteries of the voice and the window

I took the guns, but I didn't really understand why, or who we were waiting for. So I was pleased when Dupin began to explain his thoughts to me.

'Now, let's think,' he said, 'about those angry voices heard by the neighbours running up the stairs. Think about the newspaper reports of what the witnesses said. Do you remember anything *peculiar* in what they said?'

'Well,' I replied, 'all the witnesses agreed that the deep voice was that of a Frenchman. But none of them agreed about the other voice, the shrill one – they all thought something different.'

'Yes, that was what they said, but you haven't understood what's *peculiar* about it,' said Dupin. 'The peculiar thing is – not that they disagreed – but that they all thought it was the voice *of a foreigner*. Each witness thought the voice spoke a language that *they didn't know*. Look at this list.' He showed me a piece of paper.

- One Frenchman thought the voice spoke in Spanish, but *he didn't hear any words*.
- A second Frenchman thought the voice spoke in Italian, because of the sound of the words, but *he didn't know Italian himself*.

21

- A Dutchman thought the voice spoke in French, but *he himself didn't speak French.*
- An Englishman thought the voice spoke in German, but *he didn't understand German.*
- A Spaniard thought the voice spoke in English – *he couldn't speak English but he knew what it sounded like.*
- And last, an Italian thought the voice spoke in Russian, but *this man has never spoken to a Russian person.*

'So! What a strangely unusual voice this was!' said Dupin. 'Speakers of five European languages did not hear one word – not one word – that they knew. It was also a strangely shrill voice, and was it a man's voice or a woman's? No one could tell.'

'But perhaps the voice was speaking an African language,' I said. 'Or an Asian one.'

'That is always possible,' Dupin agreed, 'but do you begin to see what question we must ask next?'

Puzzled, I shook my head.

'Well, we will come back to the voice later,' said Dupin. 'But for me, my thoughts about the voice already told me what to ask next. So, let us close our eyes and remember that room on the fourth floor of the house in the Rue Morgue. What do we want to find out first? The way the murderer got out of the room. Let's think about all the possible ways. First, the door to the passage was locked, with the key on the inside. We cannot argue with a key in a locked door. There were no secret doors – the police have looked at every centimetre of the floor, the ceiling, and the walls. And I also looked very carefully. So, no secret doors. What about the chimney? It is wide enough for a body for three metres, but higher up it is much narrower. Not even a cat could climb through it to the top. So what is left?'

'The two windows,' I said. 'But they were fastened on the inside, weren't they?'

'Yes, and no,' said Dupin. 'Let me explain. We can see all of the window on the left, you remember, but only the top half of the window on the right, because the head of the bed is pushed up next to the window. The police tried to open the window on the left, but found a very strong nail in the wood, which stopped the window opening.

'They found a very strong nail in the wood.'

Another big nail was found in the other window. And the police stopped there. No one could get out of these windows, they thought, because of the nails and because both windows were fastened on the inside. So they did not try to take out the nails and open the windows.

'But I went on thinking. The windows were the only possible way, so the murderer *did* escape from one of these windows. But they were fastened on the inside, and how did the murderer fasten the window again – from the outside? There was only one answer. The window could

'After a while I found the hidden spring.'

fasten itself. I took out the nail from the window on the left, but the window still would not open. So I was sure there was a hidden spring somewhere, and after a while I found it. I pressed it, and then I could open the window.

'I put the nail back into its hole, and thought some more. The murderer gets out through the window, then the window drops down again behind him, and fastens itself by its hidden spring. But the nail – how could anybody put back the nail from the outside? I went to the other window and stood on the bed, looking down behind the bed head at the bottom half of the window. The nail in this window looked the same, but . . . There *must* be something wrong with this nail, I said to myself. I touched it – and the head of the nail came off in my fingers. The rest of the nail stayed in the wood. I carefully put back the broken nail head, pressed the hidden spring, and lifted the window a few centimetres. The nail head went up and came down with the window, but still looked like a real nail.'

'So,' I said, 'we know it was possible to escape through the window behind the bed head. But the room was on the fourth floor . . .'

'Ah,' said Dupin, 'that was the next question. You remember, don't you, how we walked around the building? And you saw, didn't you, the lightning-rod that went up the back wall of the building? And the unusual shutters on the windows on the fourth floor?'

The lightning-rod, and the unusual, latticed shutters

'Yes,' I said, 'they were like doors, but the top half was latticed, which is unusual in Paris.'

'Yes,' Dupin said, 'and very easy for a hand to get hold of. Now, let me describe a possible picture to you. The lightning-rod on the wall is less than two metres from the window by the head of the bed. The latticed shutter is more than a metre wide, and when it is open and against the wall, it is only about half a metre away from the lightning-rod. It is possible to climb up the lightning-rod to the fourth floor. Then, a strong and agile – *very* agile – person could take hold of the latticed shutter with both hands, push his feet against the wall, and swing himself and the shutter across the window. And if the window is open and this person is very agile indeed, he could swing himself into the room.'

Dupin saw the surprise in my face. 'Remember,' he said, 'that I am talking about somebody who is very strong and agile – agile in a very unusual way, perhaps. Remember also the voice, that peculiar, shrill voice, which spoke in a language that nobody knew.'

At these words I felt I almost understood what Dupin was saying. But I wasn't sure, so I said nothing and waited for him to go on explaining.

6

A madman has done this

'You will see,' my friend went on, 'that I have tried to answer another question. Not just "How did the murderer get *out of* the room?", but also "How did he get *into* it?" He used the same window both ways, I think.

'But now, let's look again at the room. You remember that on the floor there were two bags of gold, which Adolphe Le Bon carried to the house three days before. The police are so excited by this! Nearly four thousand francs in gold! Here, they say, is the motive for the murder. Well, four thousand francs in gold is a lot of money, and is certainly a *possible* motive for murder. But remember, my friend, the gold was not taken – it was still there, on the floor. So what kind of thief is that? A very, very stupid one, a thief who murders two women and then when he leaves, forgets to take the gold with him! No, no, we must forget the gold. It was not the motive for these murders.

'So far, then, the picture is like this. We have a murderer with a peculiar voice, and who is unusually agile. We have a murder without motive, a murder that is brutal and horrible even for the worst kind of criminal. How many murderers kill with their own hands, and then push the body, head downwards, up a chimney? And how strong our murderer is! He pushed the body up alone, but it took three or four people to pull it down. And think of those handfuls of long grey hair on the floor. Have you ever tried to pull hair out of someone's head? You need to be very strong to do that. You also need to be strong to cut right through someone's neck – with just a razor. And why did the old lady have so many broken bones? Because the murderer pushed her body through the open window, and it fell down onto the stones of the yard below.

'It took three or four people to pull the body down.'

'One more thing to finish the picture. Remember what the room looked like – broken chairs and tables everywhere, the mattress on the floor, nothing in its place. Now, surely, our picture is finished. What kind of murderer is so unusually strong, so unusually agile, has so peculiar a voice, kills in so brutal and horrible a way, without motive? Tell me, what is the answer?'

I felt a little ill when Dupin asked me this question. I shook my head. 'A madman,' I said, 'has done this – a wild and horrible madman, who has escaped from some hospital somewhere.'

'That is a possible answer, certainly,' Dupin replied. 'But even madmen do not have as peculiar a voice as the one heard on the stairs. Madmen speak a language of some kind. Perhaps they say strange things, but at least they speak in words. Now, there is one more thing . . .'

Dupin put his hand in his pocket and took something out. He put it on his hand and held it out to me. It was some short, orangey-brown hair.

'I took this from between the fingers of Madame L'Espanaye's hand,' he said. 'What do you make of it?'

'Dupin!' I said, astonished and afraid. 'This hair is most unusual. It is not *human* hair!'

'Did I say it was?' Dupin said. He put the hair back into his pocket, and then showed me a piece of paper. 'You remember the marks on the neck of Mademoiselle

'These marks,' I said, 'were not made by a human hand.'

L'Espanaye – marks made by the fingers that killed her?
Here is a drawing of those marks, just as they were on the
neck. Now, please put your hand on the paper, with all
your fingers in the same places as the marks.'

I tried to do this, but could not. I don't have small
hands, but my fingers were much shorter and my hand
much narrower than the marks on the drawing.

'These marks,' I said, 'were not made by a human hand.'

Dupin stood up and went to get a book from the table
behind him. He brought the book to me.

'I want you to read this page,' he said.

The page described an animal that is found in the East
Indian Islands – the orang-outang. It is a very large animal,
bigger than a man, and is strong, agile, clever, and very,

very dangerous. At once I understood just how horrible these murders were.

'Your drawing of the marks made by the fingers,' I said, 'is just as the book describes the orang-outang's hand. Also, the book describes its orangey-brown hair, which sounds just like the hair you showed me. But I still can't understand this terrible mystery. People heard *two* voices arguing – and the other voice was the voice of a Frenchman. Everybody agreed about that.'

'True,' said Dupin. 'And you will remember two of the words they heard – *Mon Dieu*. When do we say this? When we are angry, afraid, surprised, unhappy . . . I have thought about these words and made a little picture of this Frenchman, which will answer all the questions in this mystery. This is my picture. A Frenchman brings home an orang-outang from the East Indian Islands, but one night the animal escapes from him. Our Frenchman follows it through the city, trying to catch it. When the orang-outang gets into the house in the Rue Morgue, the Frenchman sees what happens, but cannot catch the animal or stop it killing the two women.

'Is this picture a true one? Of course, I don't know. But if I am right, the Frenchman himself is innocent of these murders. And if he is innocent, perhaps he will answer my advertisement. I left it at the office of *Le Monde* newspaper on our way home last night.'

Dupin gave me a piece of paper, and I read this:

CAUGHT IN THE BOIS DE BOULOGNE, early in the morning of the 4th of June, a large orang-outang, probably from the East Indian Islands. The owner, who is a sailor on a Maltese ship, can have the animal back if he comes to the following address in the Faubourg St. Germain . . .

Once again, I was astonished by what Dupin knew. 'How could you possibly know,' I asked, 'that the man was a sailor, and that he belonged to a Maltese ship?'

'I do *not* know it,' said Dupin. 'I am not *sure* of it. But I found this small piece of ribbon on the ground at the bottom of the lightning-rod. Look.'

He gave me the ribbon to look at. It was a dark-red colour, and old and dirty.

'Sailors always use ribbons like these,' Dupin said, 'to tie

'Sailors use ribbons like these to tie back their long hair.'

back their long hair. And this colour is a favourite of Maltese sailors. You see, if I am right about this, it will make the man think carefully.'

'But will he answer the advertisement?' I said. 'He saw the terrible things that his orang-outang did. Won't he be afraid to say he is its owner?'

'Yes, he will be a little afraid,' said Dupin. 'But I hope that he will think like this, and will say to himself: *I am innocent. I am poor. I can sell my orang-outang for a lot of money, and I don't want to lose that money. What danger am I in? They found the animal in the Bois de Boulogne – a long way from that house in the Rue Morgue. Who will ever know that the orang-outang did those murders? Or that I saw what happened? The police know nothing. But this advertiser knows something about me. If he wants to, he can find me easily. If I don't answer the advertisement, perhaps he will think that I have something to hide. He will start asking questions, about the animal, or about me, perhaps. No, it's better for me to answer the advertisement, get the orang-outang back, and keep the animal hidden away for a time.'*

At the very moment when Dupin stopped speaking, we heard the sound of feet on the stairs.

7
A visitor for Auguste Dupin

'Be ready with your guns,' said Dupin. 'But don't use them or show them until I say.'

The front door of the house was open, and the visitor was already half way up the stairs. The feet stopped for a moment, then began again, and a few seconds later there was a knock on the door of our room.

'Come in,' called Dupin, in a friendly way.

The door opened and a man came in. He was a sailor, clearly – a tall, strong man, with a sunburnt face. He was carrying a heavy stick, but no gun. He looked first at me, then at Dupin, and did not smile.

'Good evening,' he said.

'Sit down, my friend,' said Dupin. 'You've come about the orang-outang, yes? My word, what a fine animal that is! You're lucky to own him. Do you know how old he is?'

The sailor sat down and the worried look left his face. 'No, I don't know,' he said. 'But he's probably not more than four or five years old. Have you got him here?'

'Oh, no. We couldn't keep him in this house,' Dupin said. 'He's at a place in the Rue Dubourg, just round the corner. You can get him in the morning. Of course, you must show me that you are the real owner.'

'Yes, sir, of course,' the sailor said.

'I shall be sorry to lose the animal,' said Dupin.

'I'm very happy to pay something,' the man said. 'I know it's expensive, keeping an animal like that.'

'Well,' said my friend, 'that's good of you. What shall I ask? Let me think . . . Ah yes! This is what I want. You must tell me everything – *everything* – about these murders in the Rue Morgue.'

Dupin said these last words very quietly. Just as quietly, he walked to the door, locked it, and put the key in his pocket. He then took a gun from his coat pocket and put it, slowly and quietly, on the table in front of him.

The sailor's face turned a deep red. He jumped to his feet and took up his heavy stick. But a minute later he fell back into his chair, and sat there, shaking, with a face now as white as death itself. He said not a word. I felt deeply sorry for him.

'My friend,' said Dupin, in a kind voice, 'there's no need to be afraid – really no need. You are not in any danger from us. I know very well that you yourself are innocent of these terrible murders in the Rue Morgue. But you do know something about them. You are not a murderer, or a thief, and you have nothing to hide. But you must tell me the true story. The police have arrested an innocent man for these murders. And if you don't speak, this man will go to prison, perhaps lose his life.'

'God help me. I will tell you what I know.'

The sailor was silent for a while. Then he said, 'God help me. I will tell you what I know. You will think it's a very strange story, but it's true. I *am* innocent, and I must help this other man if I can.'

This was the sailor's story.

I have just come back from the East Indies. While I was there, I visited the island of Borneo. There I found and caught this orang-outang. It is a wild and dangerous animal, and I had a difficult journey home. But at last, we arrived back in France, and I took the animal to my house in Paris. I kept it hidden because of the neighbours, and I was planning to sell it as soon as possible for a lot of money.

On the night of the 3rd of June I was out late with some friends. When I got back home, I found the orang-outang in my bedroom, with my razor in its hand. The door to its own room was broken to pieces. I just didn't know what to do. The animal is dangerous at the best of times, but with a razor in its hands . . . ! On the ship home I always used a whip to keep the animal quiet, so I went to find my whip now. But the minute the orang-outang saw the whip, it ran out of the room, down the stairs, and jumped through an open window into the street.

I was really afraid now. How could I catch it? The animal ran, and I followed. Sometimes it stopped and looked at me, the razor still in its hand. But when I got near, it ran on again. And so we went on. Luckily, the streets were very quiet because it was nearly three o'clock in the morning.

Then, when we were going down a narrow street at the back of the Rue Morgue, the animal saw a light in a window on the fourth floor. Before I could do anything, the animal saw the lightning-rod, quickly climbed up it, took hold of the latticed shutter, and swung itself through the open window. All this took less than a minute. The shutter then swung open again, back against the wall.

'*The animal ran, and I followed.*'

At last, I thought, I can catch the animal now. But at the same time, I felt very worried. What was the animal doing in that room up there? I decided to follow it up the lightning-rod at once. When I got to the fourth floor, I found it was impossible for me to get across to the window. I could just look into the room – and at that moment a most terrible screaming began. God help me, I will never, ever forget the horrible things that I saw that night.

The orang-outang took hold of Madame L'Espanaye by the hair, with the razor still in its other hand. The daughter fainted at once, and lay still and white on the floor. The old lady tried to get away, but the animal pulled out handfuls of her hair. She fought and screamed, and this probably made it very angry. Then, with the razor, it nearly cut her head off her body. So much blood! And the blood made the animal even angrier. It ran to the girl's body and fastened its horrible hands around her neck. When she was dead, it looked up – and saw my face through the window. I was shouting at it, and it made noises back at me. Perhaps then it remembered my whip, and perhaps that's why it tried to hide the dead bodies. If you can't see anything, then nothing has happened. I don't know. First, it ran around the room, breaking all the chairs and tables, pulling the mattress off the bed. Then, it took the girl's body and pushed it up the chimney. And last, it took the old lady's body, carried it to the window, and pushed it through.

I could not watch any more. I almost fell down the lightning-rod, and ran home. I just wanted to get away from the horror of it.

❏ ❏ ❏

So that was the story behind the murders in the Rue Morgue. Just before the neighbours broke down the door of the room, the orang-outang went out through the window, which dropped down behind it.

In the end the sailor caught the orang-outang and sold it for a lot of money. We went to talk to the police inspector, and the same afternoon Adolphe Le Bon walked out of prison, a free man. The inspector was not too happy about it all. He talked a lot about people who tried to do the job of the police but who didn't understand police work.

'We won't argue with him,' Dupin said to me when we walked home together. 'Let him talk. He's a good man, in his way. I found the answer to this mystery, and he didn't. That's all there is to say, really.'

GLOSSARY

advertisement   information in a newspaper that tells you about jobs, things to buy or sell, things lost or found, etc.

agile   able to move very quickly and easily

ancient   very, very old

argue   to talk angrily with somebody because you do not agree

arrest *(v)*   when the police catch someone and take them to prison

astonished/astonishing   very, very surprised/surprising

bruise   a dark mark on your skin that comes after something hits it (*adjective*: **bruised**)

brutal   very cruel and violent

certainly   surely; without any doubt

chimney   a pipe in the wall above a fireplace, for the smoke from the fire to go up and out of the house

clearly   in a way that is easy to see, hear, or understand

clerk   a worker in an office or bank who writes letters, etc.

diable   a French word for 'devil' (a very bad person)

disagree   not to agree

drawing   a picture made with a pencil or pen

faint *(v)*   to fall down suddenly, because you are ill or afraid

fasten   to close something; to join one thing to another thing

foreigner   a person who is not from your country

horrible   very bad; making you feel afraid or sick

human *(adj & n)*   of people (not animals or machines)

impossible   not possible

innocent   if you are innocent, you have done nothing wrong

latticed   when pieces of wood, etc. cross over each other

lightning-rod   a piece of metal going down the side of a building (to take lightning safely through the building to the ground)

madman a man who is mad (ill in the head)

mattress the thick soft part of a bed

Mon Dieu French words for 'My God'; people say this when they are surprised, afraid, angry, etc.

motive a reason for doing something

nail a small thin piece of metal, which you hit into wood, to join things together

neighbour somebody who lives in the next house

orang-outang an animal like a large monkey with long arms and orangey-brown hair

owner if you are the owner of something, it belongs to you

peculiar very strange; not usual

press *(v)* to push something

probably almost certainly (you feel sure something will happen)

puzzled not able to understand or explain something

quarter a part of a town or city

razor a kind of knife, used by men to cut hair off their face

ribbon a small piece of material for tying things

shrill (of a sound) very high and loud

shutter a thing like a door which covers the outside of a window

spring *(n)* a thin piece of metal twisted round and round in the shape of many circles

swing (past tense **swung**) to move from side to side or backwards and forwards through the air

thought *(n)* something that you think

tragedy a very sad thing that happens

whip a long piece of leather or rope, for hitting animals or people

witness a person who sees something happen and can tell other people about it later

yard a piece of hard ground next to or between buildings

Before Reading

1 **Read the back cover of the book, and the introduction on the first page. How much do you know now about the story? Correct the mistakes in this passage.**

The old lady and her son were murdered on the second floor of a house in the Rue Morgue in London. The door was open, with the key on the outside of the door, and the windows were shut but not fastened. Two laughing voices were heard by friends when they ran up the stairs.

2 **Can you guess what happens in this story? Choose endings for these sentences.**

1 The murderer escaped . . .

    a) from the roof.   b) through a window.

    c) through the door.   d) down a secret stair.

2 People thought the two angry voices spoke in . . .

    a) French.   b) Russian.

    c) English.   d) French and another language.

3 The police arrested . . .

    a) a Russian sailor.   b) one of the neighbours.

    c) a bank clerk.   d) the daughter's lover.

4 The police arrested . . .

    a) the right person.   b) the wrong person.

While Reading

Read Chapter 1. How did Auguste Dupin work out what his friend was thinking? Put these notes in the right order, to show how his thinking went.

- thinking of Racine's play
- nearly falling over
- meeting the apple-seller
- looking at the street name
- Chantilly 'the new Racine'
- jumping out of the way
- turning into the Rue Racine
- hole in the street

Read Chapters 2 and 3. How much do we know now about the mystery? Which of these things are we sure about, and which are only guesses? Explain why you think this.

1 Madame L'Espanaye and her daughter lived very quietly.

2 They had no friends, and no enemies.

3 The razor was used to kill the mother.

4 The neighbours heard two voices, arguing loudly.

5 The deep voice was a man's voice, and spoke in French.

6 The shrill voice was the voice of a woman.

7 The shrill voice spoke in Italian.

8 The shrill voice spoke in Russian.

9 The murderer was very strong.

10 The murderer forgot to take the gold when he left.

11 The murderer was not interested in the gold.

Before you read Chapter 4, can you guess what Auguste Dupin will do next? Choose some of these ideas.

Auguste Dupin will . . .

1 talk to all the witnesses again.
2 ask some clever questions.
3 visit all the neighbours' houses.
4 look for a heavy piece of wood.
5 visit the Rue Morgue and look carefully at the room.
6 tell the police the murderer's name.

Read Chapters 4 and 5, and join these halves of sentences.

1 The police arrested Adolphe Le Bon . . .
2 Dupin was waiting for a visitor . . .
3 The witnesses agreed about the deep voice, . . .
4 The witnesses all thought that the shrill voice was the voice of a foreigner, . . .
5 The windows were fastened with nails on the inside, . . .
6 An agile person could climb up the lightning-rod . . .

7 but they did not agree which language it spoke.
8 which they said was the voice of a Frenchman.
9 probably because they thought he wanted to steal the four thousand francs.
10 and swing into the room through the open window.
11 who knew something about the murders.
12 but the nail in the right window was broken.

Before you read Chapter 6, how much can you guess about the mystery? Think about these questions.

1 Is Dupin right about the window and the lightning-rod? Is there another way of escaping from the room?

2 The narrator isn't sure that he understands. What is Dupin trying to tell him?

Read Chapter 6. How did these things help Dupin to find the answer? Explain what he was thinking for each thing.

1 the four thousand francs in gold
2 the handfuls of long grey hair
3 the peculiar voice
4 the short, orangey-brown hair
5 the old, dirty dark-red ribbon
6 the Bois de Boulogne

Before you read Chapter 7, can you guess how the story ends? Choose as many answers as you like.

1 The sailor . . .

   a) tries to run away.   b) tells Dupin the true story.

   c) is sent to prison.   d) is the real murderer.

2 The orang-outang . . .

   a) is never found.   b) kills two more people.

   c) is shot and killed.   d) is sold for a lot of money.

After Reading

1 **What did Dupin say to the police inspector at the end? Put their conversation in the right order, and write in the speakers' names. Dupin speaks first (number 3).**

1 _____ 'But I know how to think. I know what questions to ask. And you'll find my answer is right.'

2 _____ 'A *WHAT*?'

3 _____ 'I have come to tell you, Inspector, the answer to the Rue Morgue mystery.'

4 _____ 'Oh, will I? What makes you so sure?'

5 _____ 'An orang-outang. It escaped from its owner's house with a razor, and climbed into the room through the window.'

6 _____ 'But we already know the answer, Dupin. The bank clerk murdered the women for the money.'

7 _____ 'Because I have a witness – who was outside the window on the lightning-rod, and who saw it all.'

8 _____ 'An orang-outang with a razor? Listen, Dupin, don't try to do my job for me. You don't know anything about police work.'

9 _____ 'No, he didn't. Adolphe Le Bon is an innocent man. The killer was an orang-outang from Borneo.'

2 Here is a new illustration for the story. Find the best place in the story to put the picture, and answer these questions.

The picture goes on page _____.

1 Where is the sailor?

2 Why is he shouting?

3 What does he do next, and why?

Now write a caption for the illustration.

Caption: _____

49

3 Here are some more newspaper stories from the *Gazette*. Use the words below to complete the stories. (Use each word once.)

agile, arrested, bank, belongs, caught, dropped, escaped, feet, free, hands, horrible, how, hurt, into, motive, out of, outside, same, sell, shutter, thousand, through, up, which, who

STORY ONE

Adolphe Le Bon, _____ works for Mignaud & Son as a _____ clerk, today left prison, a _____ man. The police _____ him because they thought that the _____ for the murders was the four _____ francs in gold, _____ Le Bon carried to the house for Madame L'Espanaye. 'But it was all a _____ mistake,' said a friend of Le Bon's. 'Adolphe couldn't _____ a fly.'

STORY TWO

The police now know _____ the murderer got _____ and _____ the room in the house in the Rue Morgue. He climbed _____ the lightning-rod on the wall _____, and took hold of the open _____ with both _____. Then he pushed his _____ against the wall and swung himself into the room _____ the open window. He went out the _____ way, and the window _____ down behind him.

STORY THREE

Early this morning an orang-outang was _____ in the Bois de Boulogne. The animal, which comes from Borneo,

_____ to a sailor and _____ from his house four days ago. It is a large animal, and is strong, _____, and very dangerous. The sailor is planning to _____ it as soon as he can.

4 **Now write a fourth story for the newspaper, saying what really happened. You could begin like this:**

At last we have the answer to the brutal Rue Morgue murders. The two women were killed by . . .

5 **Here are some headlines for the newspaper stories. Choose the best headline for each of the four stories.**

ASTONISHING ANSWER TO RUE MORGUE TRAGEDY

POLICE ARRESTED INNOCENT MAN

WILD ANIMAL FOUND IN CITY PARK

KEEP YOUR SHUTTERS CLOSED AT NIGHT!

6 **After the fourth story, some people wrote letters to the newspapers. Do you agree with any of them? Explain why.**

1 'Why is this animal still alive? It killed two innocent women. Someone must shoot it at once!'

2 'The sailor must go to prison. The animal belonged to him and he let it escape. He must not make any money from selling it.'

3 'It is wrong to bring a wild animal to a city. The orang-outang's home is in Borneo and it must go back there.'

ABOUT THE AUTHOR

Edgar Allan Poe was born in 1809 in Boston, USA. His parents died when he was young, and he went to live with the Allan family in Richmond. He spent a year at university, and then two years in the army. In 1831 he moved to Baltimore, where he lived with his aunt and his cousin Virginia. For the next few years life was difficult; he wrote stories and sold them to magazines, but it brought him little money. But he did find happiness with Virginia, whom he married in 1836.

From 1838 to 1844 Poe lived in Philadelphia. Here he wrote some of his most famous stories, such as *The Fall of the House of Usher* and *The Pit and the Pendulum*. Then he moved to New York City, where his poem *The Raven* soon made him famous. But Virginia died in 1847, and Poe began drinking heavily. He tried to kill himself in 1848, and died the following year.

Poe is best known for his horror stories, but he also wrote poetry, funny stories, mysteries, and stories about time travel – a kind of early science fiction. He is often called the father of the modern detective story, because of his story *The Murders in the Rue Morgue*. It was the first story to show how the detective thinks, and because of this the Mystery Writers of America give a prize called an 'Edgar' to the writer of the best mystery each year. There have been several films of this famous story. A silent film in 1914 was followed by two more films, both of which told a completely different story from the original. A film made for television in 1986 was much closer to Poe's story.

OXFORD BOOKWORMS LIBRARY

Classics • Crime & Mystery • Factfiles • Fantasy & Horror
Human Interest • Playscripts • Thriller & Adventure
True Stories • World Stories

The OXFORD BOOKWORMS LIBRARY provides enjoyable reading in English, with a wide range of classic and modern fiction, non-fiction, and plays. It includes original and adapted texts in seven carefully graded language stages, which take learners from beginner to advanced level. An overview is given on the next pages.

All Stage 1 titles are available as audio recordings, as well as over eighty other titles from Starter to Stage 6. All Starters and many titles at Stages 1 to 4 are specially recommended for younger learners. Every Bookworm is illustrated, and Starters and Factfiles have full-colour illustrations.

The OXFORD BOOKWORMS LIBRARY also offers extensive support. Each book contains an introduction to the story, notes about the author, a glossary, and activities. Additional resources include tests and worksheets, and answers for these and for the activities in the books. There is advice on running a class library, using audio recordings, and the many ways of using Oxford Bookworms in reading programmes. Resource materials are available on the website <www.oup.com/elt/gradedreaders>.

The *Oxford Bookworms Collection* is a series for advanced learners. It consists of volumes of short stories by well-known authors, both classic and modern. Texts are not abridged or adapted in any way, but carefully selected to be accessible to the advanced student.

You can find details and a full list of titles in the *Oxford Bookworms Library Catalogue* and *Oxford English Language Teaching Catalogues*, and on the website <www.oup.com/elt/gradedreaders>.

THE OXFORD BOOKWORMS LIBRARY
GRADING AND SAMPLE EXTRACTS

STARTER • 250 HEADWORDS

present simple – present continuous – imperative –
can/cannot, must – *going to* (future) – simple gerunds …

Her phone is ringing – but where is it?

Sally gets out of bed and looks in her bag. No phone. She looks under the bed. No phone. Then she looks behind the door. There is her phone. Sally picks up her phone and answers it. *Sally's Phone*

STAGE 1 • 400 HEADWORDS

… past simple – coordination with *and, but, or* –
subordination with *before, after, when, because, so* …

I knew him in Persia. He was a famous builder and I worked with him there. For a time I was his friend, but not for long. When he came to Paris, I came after him – I wanted to watch him. He was a very clever, very dangerous man. *The Phantom of the Opera*

STAGE 2 • 700 HEADWORDS

… present perfect – *will* (future) – *(don't) have to, must not, could* –
comparison of adjectives – simple *if* clauses – past continuous –
tag questions – *ask/tell* + infinitive …

While I was writing these words in my diary, I decided what to do. I must try to escape. I shall try to get down the wall outside. The window is high above the ground, but I have to try. I shall take some of the gold with me – if I escape, perhaps it will be helpful later. *Dracula*

STAGE 3 • 1000 HEADWORDS

… should, may – present perfect continuous – *used to* – past perfect –
causative – relative clauses – indirect statements …

Of course, it was most important that no one should see
Colin, Mary, or Dickon entering the secret garden. So Colin
gave orders to the gardeners that they must all keep away
from that part of the garden in future. **The Secret Garden**

STAGE 4 • 1400 HEADWORDS

… past perfect continuous – passive (simple forms) –
would conditional clauses – indirect questions –
relatives with *where/when* – gerunds after prepositions/phrases …

I was glad. Now Hyde could not show his face to the world
again. If he did, every honest man in London would be proud
to report him to the police. **Dr Jekyll and Mr Hyde**

STAGE 5 • 1800 HEADWORDS

… future continuous – future perfect –
passive (modals, continuous forms) –
would have conditional clauses – modals + perfect infinitive …

If he had spoken Estella's name, I would have hit him. I was so
angry with him, and so depressed about my future, that I could
not eat the breakfast. Instead I went straight to the old house.
Great Expectations

STAGE 6 • 2500 HEADWORDS

… passive (infinitives, gerunds) – advanced modal meanings –
clauses of concession, condition

When I stepped up to the piano, I was confident. It was as if I
knew that the prodigy side of me really did exist. And when I
started to play, I was so caught up in how lovely I looked that
I didn't worry how I would sound. **The Joy Luck Club**

Sherlock Holmes Short Stories

SIR ARTHUR CONAN DOYLE

Retold by Clare West

Sherlock Holmes is the greatest detective of them all. He sits in his room, and smokes his pipe. He listens, and watches, and thinks. He listens to the steps coming up the stairs; he watches the door opening – and he knows what question the stranger will ask.

In these three of his best stories, Holmes has three visitors to the famous flat in Baker Street – visitors who bring their troubles to the only man in the world who can help them.

The Pit and the Pendulum and Other Stories

EDGAR ALLAN POE

Retold by John Escott

Everybody has bad dreams, when horrible things move towards you in the dark, things you can hear but not see. Then you wake up, in your own warm bed, and turn over to go back to sleep.

But suppose you wake up on a hard prison floor, in a darkness blacker than the blackest night. You hear the sound of water, you touch a cold metal wall, and smell a wet dead smell. Death is all around you, waiting …

In these stories by Edgar Allan Poe, death whispers at you from every dark corner, and fear can drive you mad …